The Best is Yet to COME

The Best is Yet to COME

Della Jane Buckley

Copyright © 2020 by Della Jane Buckley.

Library of Congress Control Number:		2020920189
ISBN:	Hardcover	978-1-6641-3659-5
	Softcover	978-1-6641-3657-1
	eBook	978-1-6641-3658-8

All rights reserved. No part of this book may be reproduced or transmitted in any form or by any means, electronic or mechanical, including photocopying, recording, or by any information storage and retrieval system, without permission in writing from the copyright owner.

Scripture quotations marked KJV are from the Holy Bible, King James Version (Authorized Version). First published in 1611. Quoted from the KJV Classic Reference Bible, Copyright © 1983 by The Zondervan Corporation.

Any people depicted in stock imagery provided by Getty Images are models, and such images are being used for illustrative purposes only.
Certain stock imagery © Getty Images.

Print information available on the last page.

Rev. date: 10/13/2020

To order additional copies of this book, contact:
Xlibris
844-714-8691
www.Xlibris.com
Orders@Xlibris.com
820647

Credits: Special thanks to my parents-Deacon Andrew Jackson and Ora Belle Johnson Buckley, Betty Sue Buckley Pace, MD-Forward, Dr. James Kinchen-Editor and Bishop Lawrence L Kirby, Senior Pastor and Mentor at St. Paul Missionary Baptist Church in Racine, Wisconsin. My deep love and compassion to my three children, Yusuf Ali-First Born, Tiffany Racquel-Only Daughter and Tyrone Bashsir-Baby Boy for your sincere love and support. God has allowed our journey to developed over many years of love, hurt and the comfort of being REAL! May the Lord continue to bless each of you with much Grace and Hope!

Contents

Foreword ix

About the Author xiii

Holiness Or Hell 1

Due Season 3

Faith & Favor Of God 9

Peace 17

Real Love 21

A Tribute of Love 33

Foreword

The three-part series, Royal Della Jane's Journey of Life chronicles her life from childhood to the revelation of our family interactions that shaped the way forward into inspired revelation, *The Best Is Yet to Come*! Go ahead, preach and teach the gospel to all that would hear "the good news of Jesus Christ". As the seventh born of patriarch Andrew Jackson and matriarch Ora Bell Johnson-Buckley, Della Jane has taken on the leadership and "matriarch" role. Her dedication over the years has kept the Buckley family together for better or worse after daddy's sudden passing on April 2, 1999. Della's continued daring efforts through the Daughters of Zion Ministry, gave us the gift of the only beautiful photograph preserved of our parents. I thank God for Della and what she has sustained over the years. Yet she rises to the task at hand, not always perfect, but faithful to get it done. It is important to give credit for "good works" despite differences in opinions, because when the "rubber meets the road" who will be left in the dust? As we all are coming through our personal journeys inspired by this three-part series, we should all be inspired to be as open to help others, struggling with the same issues. I thank God for brave women willing to tell their story, which is needed in our times of chaos and unrest in our nation and the world. In the words of the late Maya Angelou *"And Still I Rise"*. Sister Della ….be strong in the Lord and in the power of His might. Put on the whole armor of God, that you may be able to stand against the wiles of the devil. (*Ephesians 6:10-11*). God Bless You.

With loving kindness and respect,

Betty Sue Buckley-Pace
Your sister
Tenth born of fifteen

Andrew Jackson Buckley
07/26/1920 – 04/02/1999
Ora Bell Johnson-Buckley
03/05/1923 – 08/03/1992

"Royal Della Jane's Journey of Life Uncensored" was released in March 2020. The preceding book, Royal Della Jane's Journey of Life (Christian Publisher) was released on February 4, 2010. Now here we are in August 2020, ten years later and I am releasing the second and last account of this journey. "The Best is Yet to Come." My present state of mind is in emotional turmoil but striving to be hopeful knowing that God works all things for my good. I know the best is yet to come but, I am facing the fight of my life, breast cancer. I am scheduled for radiation followed by chemotherapy. I do not want to experience these two treatments, nevertheless, I am going to the Cancer Center by request of the two cancer treatment physicians and with Jesus' covering!

In my present state of mind, I am compelled to release this publication including a variety of sermons that I have written and preached in Racine and Kenosha, Wisconsin Community Churches. I am blessed to say that Bishop Lawrence L. Kirby licensed and ordained me as a minister of the Gospel Preaching Ministry. It is amazing how God allows you to embrace your destiny and touch various people in the church and community to help lead you to proclaim and embrace your God given destiny... my preaching ministry. Through the preaching ministry God birthed the Daughters of Zion Ministry that honors my parents, the late Deacon Andrew Jackson, and late Ora Belle Johnson Buckley.

Every year since 2007, we have an annual recognition celebration to honor my family and others in the Racine Community. Throughout the years, God has anointed and appointed me to be a carrier of the Good News of Jesus Christ throughout the world. Jesus said, "Go ye therefore into all the world baptizing them in the name of the Father, Son and the Holy Ghost…In Jesus Name!

In Royal Della Jane's Journey of Life Uncensored, author Minister Della Jane Buckley, brings a much-needed *grab-you-by-the-shoulders* moment of real talk, filled with entertaining stories, profanity, and ruthless humor. This manifestation is a refreshing slap in the face for all of us, so that we can start to lead more contented, grounded lives.

When I wrote the first book on February 24, 2010, Della Jane had all her real experiences included but the publisher removed some because they are a Christian Publisher. This time around, I included profanity and very unpleasant vulvar experiences, not to offend you, but to expose how this has helped me grow by *grace* over the years. For the past ten years, my friends remarked to me, you have not told the full story of her life's experiences. So, after many years of debate and agony, I came to the reality of what the hell, just tell the Uncensored truth. Della Jane's mother would always say, "Bitch, just tell the truth." So, in the author's own words: Here's the real deal. I know this is going to be a shocker to the entire community and particularly the church community, but I wanted to put this out there. This version might help save a life."

About the Author

Della Jane Buckley is the seventh child born to the late Deacon Andrew Jackson and Ora Belle Johnson Buckley. Della Jane accepted the Lord as her savior at the age of twelve. She is the mother to Yusuf, Tiffany, and Tyrone. Della Jane is a licensed and ordained minister at St. Paul Missionary Baptist Church under the leadership of Bishop Lawrence L. Kirby. She received a BA in Mass Communication from the University of Wisconsin-Parkside. She received clergy training from the Bible Institute of St. Paul Missionary Baptist Church in Racine, Wisconsin, under the instruction of Bishop Lawrence L. Kirby, MA, BA. Della Jane is the Founder/CEO of the Daughters of Zion

Ministry. From past experiences with poverty, isolation and loneliness, Della Jane learned to take advantage of different circumstances to rise from the ashes like a phoenix with renewed determination to walk out her preordained destiny. As the seventh child out of fifteen children, Della Jane came into her unique personality early on, which became the driving force for many of the decisions made as a teen and young adult. Della's journey, although a tortuous path, led her ultimately to become an ordained minister and founder of the Daughters of Zion Ministry. Through this anointed ministry, Della Jane has embraced her destiny and finds great joy in passing on the wisdom acquired over the years to help young women and men find their rightful place in society.

Holiness Or Hell

Holiness or wholeness of heart and life is the inevitable outcome of an experience with God when He purifies our very natures from all sin. "Follow peace with all men, and holiness without which no man shall see the Lord." Hebrews 12:14. Jesus said somewhat the same thing in Matthew 5:8, "Blessed are the pure in heart: for they shall see God." There is no room for sin in the heart that has been made pure by the Spirit of God.

Shame on those who profess to belong to Christ and still contend they must sin and confess and again sin and confess. Let everyone that Namath the name of Christ "DEPARTS" from iniquity, (2Timothy 2:19). They have perverted the truth and the Word of god has become of none effect to them. Sin separates man from God and condemns him to everlasting punishment in HELL, as the penalty. Sinning "Christians" are a by-product of man-made religion and have no foundation in the Word of God. Listen to 1 Peter 1:15-16, "But as he which hath called you is holy, so BE YE holy in all manner of conversation; because it is written, be ye holy for I am holy." Again, in Ephesians 1:4 we read, "According as he hath chosen us in him before the foundation of the world that we should be holy and without blame before him in love." In the light of these forgoing scriptures, and many more that could be brought to bear on the subject, it is plain to see that God's true people today are a holy people as God is Holy!

"Heaven is a holy place, filled with glory and with grace. Sin can never enter there. If you cling to sin till death, when you draw your last breath, you will sink in dark despair to the regions of the lost. Thus, to prove at an awful cost—Sin can never enter there."

The moral standard for New Testament Christians is holiness. Each one of us is traveling on one road or the other right now. The road to heaven is described as the highway of holiness in Isaiah 35:8. By contrast, the road to hell is pictured as a broad, wide road leading down to destruction (Matthew 7:13). My dear friend, which road are you on today?

Due Season

Galatians 6: 9: "And let us not be weary in well doing: for in due season we shall reap, if we faint not."

Today we live in a society that is fast forward. For example, fast food restaurants, drive thru, cell phones, or cable television. We stay in the mind-set, "I want it NOW!" We have grown into a "NOW" mentality. We are so conditioned by technology. The old way is not good enough. We are set in a fast forward mentality. No patience! Instead, we have a "quick and faster" mentality.

In the Bible, Christians are called to endure trials and tribulations. Jesus's suffering is our perfect example of endurance. The outcome of our endurance is spiritual reward. Believers will experience periods of doubt on their journey. It may seem that your works are for naught or that God has forgotten us.

We will often cry out to the Lord in despair. "Lord have

mercy!" We often grow weary. We quickly become discouraged. We must continue to press our way despite what it looks like. We must tread forward. We must continue to move forward.

I. Weary

Do not grow weary in your due season. What does weary mean? Mental and physical exhaustion, impatience; being dissatisfied.

"Even youths grow tired and weary, and young men stumble and fall; but those who wait on the Lord will renew their strength. They will soar on wings like eagles. They will run and not grow weary." Isaiah 40:31 We always criticize ourselves time after time. We tend to be hard on ourselves never satisfied with what we have accomplished. We always want more and more. When we come to church, we will put on the church look, the fake faces.

The devil always plays tricks on our minds. Stop it! Look at the positive things in life. We all fall short, but the Lord looks beyond our shortcomings and looks at our hearts.

God wants us to realize that he has placed a treasure within us. Stop this mentality, "I will fake it until I make it." The Devil is a lie! Tell yourself, "I can do all things through Christ that strengthens me."

Stop being the "dirt inspector." Stop looking at the negative and how we fall short. "*All* have sinned and come short of the glory of God." Whatever you must face in life, face it with the power of God. We do not believe in ourselves. The power is in the Lord.

Whatever you have got to face, face it in the power of our Lord God. Listen! It is not about me. It is not about you. This battle is not ours; it is the Lord's. Stop looking at the negatives in our lives. God has placed a treasure inside of us. The power is in the Lord. We must realize that we are messengers from God. We must operate in His strength. Stop being weary. Stop trying to handle it in y our own strength. God says, "I want you to handle it in *my* strength!" Face your challenges in the strength of Almighty God. Stand and see the salvation of the Lord. God says, "I will never leave you nor forsake you... Just STAND!"

"My hope is built on nothing less than Jesus love and righteousness." We must ignite our hope mentality. With this hope we must have faith and feel that all things are possible to them that believe. God knows our needs. Do not grow weary in well doing for in due season we will reap if we faint not. Just think about our fore parents that endured so many hardships. But they continue to put their trust in God. For God I live and for God I die.

II. Unforgotten Works

There will be periods in this life when it seems your good works are for naught. Or it might appear that God has forgotten and does not care. We often grow weary and become discouraged. We may be faced with opposition. "Be not dismayed, whatever betide, God will take care of you." In due season we will reap if we faint not. Do not give up, do not give in. Help is on the way. In due season we shall reap if we do not lose heart and give up.

The question is implied: "In what respect?" and the answer: "if we don't grow weary." The dangers that we face are the opposition to good. We are faced with outward hindrances. We are faced with opposition to good. Do not throw in the towel. We will reap if we faint not. We may not be what we ought to be, but we can change. We will reap if we do not lost heart and give up. Have faith! Without faith it is impossible to please God. Let us not grow weary. The weariness arises from the opposition to good.

The outward hindrances are from the naysayers and the Prosecution. We often will prosecute the naysayers consciously and unconsciously. We are so quick to give out our choices of others. Often, we need to look in the mirror. It is me Oh Lord standing in the need of deliverance. My father would always tell me, "Gal, hold your tongue. You talk too much." Glory be unto God for the grace that is furnished by Christ Jesus, our Lord and Savior. If we would allow Jesus to correct us and be serious about our lives, we would be much better. It is me oh Lord stand in the need of prayer. Let us stop looking at others outward sign and focus on our inward faults, we can be much better individuals. Why not start today. Matter of fact start right now!

We shall reap if we faint not. If we do not give in or over to being exhausted and disheartened, we will be winners. We must persevere to receive our rewards from God. We must make a pledge to do well despite the weariness. We must continue to pledge to serve God with a cheerful Heart. We must keep our eyes on the prize. For God we live, for God we die. We must keep our eyes on the prize!

There is always a cause and effect outcome. Every action has a consequence. We are the sum of our actions. I am going to sow to the Spirit. What about you? Eternal life awaits those who are willing to sow to the Spirit by patiently doing the right thing. Patiently continue in well doing, always seeking God's glory and immorality. Seek eternal life. Our due season is coming. Do not give up. Do not give in. Do not give out. I am going to trust in the Lord until I die. I am going to stay on the battlefield until I die. Do not be weary. Do not faint. Your due season is coming. Your due season is NOW! All we have is now. Yesterday is gone. We all are hoping for tomorrow. All we have is NOW!

I am going to sow to the Spirit. What about you? Eternal life awaits those who are willing to sow to the Spirit by patiently doing the right thing. Patiently continuing in well doing. Seek God's glory and honor and immorality. Seek Eternal Life NOW!!

Ponder your Thoughts

Faith & Favor Of God

Romans 1:17. "For in the gospel a righteousness from God is revealed, a righteousness that is by faith from first to last, just as it is written: the righteous shall live by faith."

Our salvation comes as a gift of God's grace. It can only be appropriated or set aside by the human response of faith. To understand the process of salvation, we must understand Saving Faith. Faith in Jesus is the only condition God requires for salvation. One must profess and acknowledge Jesus Christ as Lord and Savior. "If thou shall confess with thy mouth the Lord Jesus and believe in thy heart that God raised Him from the dead, thou shall be saved." Romans 10:9 Saving Faith is also an activity coming from our hearts. This heart activity compels one to be a seeker and to follow Jesus Christ as Lord and Savior.

Let us examine New Testament Faith.

Faith as presented in the New Testament means believing firmly and trusting in the crucified and risen Christ as your personal savior. Is Jesus your personal savior? "Personal" means an imitate relationship with Jesus Christ. Believing with your whole heart. The heart involves the will, the emotion, and the intellect. One must trust God and die to your carnal man – your fleshly-self. Your will of being and thinking must die. One must die to the flesh. The mind – your own way of thinking- must die.

God tells us to get wisdom and to get understanding. But this wisdom and understanding does not come from the world. Reading, studying, meditating, and praying on God's word gives us the foundation to train our minds to die to self. Our individual minds often hinder us from receiving God's favor. We are embodied in a "my, me and I" mentality. *I* think, *I* will, *I* cannot, *I* will not...this is a familiar pattern of the human will. Bring *me my* this and *my* that... get off *my* couch... close *my* refrigerator, this is *my* car, etc. My mother told me early in life I should stop saying my, my, me. Nothing is mines. It all belongs to God. God has just entrusted us to be stewards over it. Is this your mental attitude? Check yourself. The word, "you," is another good word used out of context for God... *you* do this, *you* do that. When you use the "you" word in the wrong content, it puts you in a command post. Often pointing the finger when the "you" word is uttering it out of our mouths too often. We must train and teach our minds to put away old habits that can hinder our walk with God. Old habits die hard. The mind is a complex organism that must be taught to die. One must operate in the spirit of John 4:24. "God is Spirit and His worshippers must worship Him in spirit and truth."

Jesus Christ is *truth*. To live in union with Christ, one must speak the truth. God despises a liar. To claim to have fellowship with Christ and to possess salvation, yet not live and speak according to the truth is a stench in God's nostrils. You do *not* want to be a stench! What is a stench? Something having a foul smell. Are our attitudes and behavior a stench? Think of a skunk. Now that is a stench. Our expressions and reactions that we show towards each other are often stinky, rotten stenches. Those who have no truth in them show the real conditions of their hearts. They are stenches before God. Simply, such a person is in opposition with God. You are *outside* the kingdom of God. All those that say, "Lord, Lord," will not enter the kingdom of heaven. God tells us to seek the kingdom of Heaven. "Seek ye first the kingdom of God and His righteousness and all these things will be added onto you." (Matthew 6:33)

Remember the New Testament Faith.

Faith means passionately believing and trusting in the crucified and risen Christ as our personal Lord and Savior. Romans 1:17 says, "For in the gospel a righteousness from God is revealed, a righteousness that is by faith, from first to last, just as it is written, the righteous will live by faith." It involves believing with all our whole heart. Romans 6:17 reminds us that Christianity demands "obedience from the heart to Godly standards." Here we go again with the *heart* principle – the will, the emotion, and the intellect. You cannot "talk Christ" with lip service only. It must be lived out. Walk it out! Our hearts cannot be far from the truth. Even in this day of grace, saints must remain under God's instructions, discipline and duty of obeying Christ's law and His word.

Faith in operation. Obedience to Jesus Christ and His word as the only way of life comes from faith. Romans 1:5 tells us, "Through Him and for his name's sake, we received grace and apostleship to call people from among the Gentiles to the obedience that comes from faith." This is a joining of one's life to God through Jesus Christ in love, devotion, gratitude, and obedience. Faith and obedience are inseparable, ultimately, leading to sanctification. We must be sanctified and set apart, for without holiness no one can enter the Kingdom of God. Grace is God's presence and love through Christ Jesus. It is given to all born-again believers by the Holy Spirit. The Holy Spirit imparts mercy, forgiveness, desire, and power to do God's will. A Christian's life from the beginning to the end is dependent on God's grace. God gives a measure of grace to unbelievers so that they can be able to believe in the Lord Jesus Christ. Titus 2:11 declares, "For the grace of God that brings salvation has appeared to all people." God gives grace to believers to have set them free from sin. Romans 6:20 says, "When you were slaves to sin, you were free from the control of righteousness." Romans 6:22 assures, "But now that you have been set free from sin and have become slaves to God, the benefits you reap leads to holiness and the result is eternal life."

Here we go again. Holiness.

God's grace must be diligently desired and sought. Hebrews 4:16 declares, "Let us then approach the throne of grace with confidence so that we may receive mercy and find grace to help us in our time of need. Faith involves repentance. Repent, truly sorrowfully turning from sin. God commands all people everywhere to repent. There are no exceptions. God will not overlook any one's sins. All must turn from sin or be condemned. Condemned where? – eternal punishment, Hell! Repentance is essential to receiving salvation. "Choose ye this day whom you will serve." Who are you going to serve? Faith involve turning to God through Jesus Christ. No man can come unto the Father unless they come through Jesus Christ. "Repent for the kingdom of God is at hand." Matthew 3:2. It is right now! Repent basically means to turn around. It is like a car doing a U-turn. It may have been headed north, but after making the U-turn, it is now going south – in the opposite direction. It is turning *from* evil ways and turning *to* Christ and through Jesus *to* God. In John 14:1, Jesus informs us, "Do not let your heart be troubled, trust in God, trust also in me." In verse six of the same passage, Jesus continues, "I am the way and the truth and the life. No one comes to the Father except through (by) me." Jesus is the way! In Matthew 11:28-29, He says, " Come to me all who labor and are heavy laden and I will give you rest. Take my yoke upon you and learn from me."

Straight is the gate. Come straight way right now. Come right now while the blood is running warm through your veins.

Repentance is *free,* enabled by Grace through hearing the gospel of Jesus Christ. God sympathizes with us. We can approach His throne with our weakness, concerns, joys, and love. It's called the Throne of Grace because God's love flows down to us. Not only His love, but His help, mercy, forgiveness, spiritual powers, out-pouring of the Holy Spirit, spiritual gifts, and the fruits of the Spirit. It flows forever and ever. Do not let the devil fool you. Do not resist God's grace. Hebrew 12:15 warns, "See to it that no one misses the grace of God and that no bitter root grows up to cause trouble and defile, causing many bitter roots," attitudes of animosity and bitter resentment. This is another sermon all by itself. Do not let bitterness enter your heart. Faith opens the door to favor. God's favor gives us something when our faith does not have time to manifest it.

Lastly, faith has no fears.

Faith operates in blindness. You cannot expect the eyes to see the faith in operation but you must have the faith to believe it. "If I can't see it, I can't believe it" is a trick of the Devil. Get out of the way of God. You cannot figure it out. God has already worked it out. Count it as already *done!* It is a *Done Deal!*

Hebrews 11:1 King James Version (KJV) 11 Now faith is the substance of things hoped for, the evidence of things not seen. The Bible says that faith gives substance to the things you hope for. In other words, faith brings those things into your life. The basic definition of faith, according to the Bible, is simply believing in God's goodness and believing that He rewards the people who seek after Him.

God's favor, or grace, is God giving us the ability to do something which is humanly impossible for us to do. God's favor is for a purpose. When He favors you, it is not for you to sit upon, but to do something with. You receive blessing so you can be a blessing!

What does have favor means? To prefer (someone) especially in an unfair way: to show that you like or approve of (someone) more than others: to approve of or support (something): to regard (someone or something) as most likely to succeed or win. In Psalm 90:17: Let the favor of the Lord our God be upon us and establish the work of our hands upon us; yes, establish the work of our hands! Proverbs 12:2: A good man obtains favor from the Lord, but a man of evil devices he condemns.

Faith is an awesome Blessing that is obtained from the Almighty GOD; EL-SHADDAI. It is part of an inheritance based upon what JESUS did for us. Supernatural Favor is additionally, a privilege, a special right, benefit, or advantage.

How to Activate Divine Favor:

1. Life of obedience do whatever God says, God favors those who are obedient and careful to obey Him (Deuteronomy 28:1-2)
2. Walk righteously- Psalms 5:12 "For thou, LORD, wilt bless the righteous; with favor wilt thou compass him as *with* a shield."

3. Sow into the life of a favored person - Hebrews 7:6. "But he whose descent is not counted from them received tithes of Abraham and blessed him that had the promises."
4. Place value on prophetic anointing and grace upon your life.

Lift your hand by faith and grace. Ask God for grace and God will bring it into existence. Grace is God' s unmerited favor. Favor, we do not deserve it. Favor is not fair. Think of faith as the slow postal carrier of your vision and favor of UPS next day delivery. Favor may not come when you want Him. He is always right on time. When you purpose in life to please God, good things will come into your life. Favor, Favor, Favor

Peace

1 Peter 3:11: "Let him turn away from evil, and do good; let him seek peace, and pursue it."

Today we live in a society that does not talk about peace. We are busy with the ins and outs of survival. We are bombarded with things, bills, health issues, and the list goes on and on. We are constantly crying out to God for deliverance.

We need the Lordship of God over and in our lives. The Bible tells us God will keep us in *perfect peace* if we keep our mind on Him. Today, I want to explore peace. How do you seek peace? The Bible tells us in 1 Peter 3:11 to turn away from wickedness. "Let him eschew evil, and do good; let him seek peace, and ensue it." Shun evil or shun any appearance of sin. We are encouraged to do the right thing. When I try to do right, evil is forever present. When was the last time you searched for peace? Searched for harmony, undisturbed from fear? When did you go after peace that surpasses all understanding? Today I challenge you to let go of your worries. When you do this, you become supernaturally relaxed. Rediscover the peace that surpasses all understanding. Be at peace with yourself. Stop worrying!

Matthew 6:33 says, "Seek ye first the kingdom of God." The promise is made if we seek Him first and the righteousness of His kingdom, all earthly things will be supplied. Now is the time to seek God first. We seek everything first but God. Seek ye first the kingdom of God and all these things will be added unto thee.

The promise is made that if we seek Jesus first, and the righteousness of His kingdom, all earthly wants will be supplied. The kingdom of God is universal, including all moral intelligences. We should willingly surrender to the will of God. The kingdom of God is inward and spiritual. We must be in the right state of heart and mind, soul, and spirit.

Let go of worry. We worry too much and trust God too little. Rediscover the peace of God. Strive for calmness in your life.

1 Corinthians 1:30 tells us, "But of him are ye in Christ Jesus, who of God is made unto us wisdom, and righteousness, and sanctification, and redemption." Jesus is the source of all wisdom. God gave us a divine plan of salvation through Jesus Christ our Lord and Savior. This makes us upright with Him, making us pure and holy.

Jesus paid for our redemption. Jesus is everything we need in any situation. Jesus is *everything* we need in any situation! He is sufficient to meet every need for every circumstance. The Bible tells us to watch and pray. Immediately start praying. Do not wait, PRAY! Apply the blood of Jesus by faith to every situation. Jesus is our Passover Lamb. Jesus passed over from death to life. Remember Jesus defeated Satan at Calvary's cross. Be aggressive with the Devil. Do not wait! Do not be a procrastinator. Should have, could have is not good enough. Do not wait. Resist the Devil at the onset. Stir yourself up in the Holy Ghost. Fan your inner fire within you. Take your life and go forward. Do not let Satan get the VICTORY! There will be peace, oh peace! Whenever the Lord says peace, there will peace. Fan your inner fire. Take your life and go forward. Do not let Satan get the Victory! There will be peace, oh peace! Whenever the Lord says peace there will be PEACE!

Faith is believing in Jesus. Jesus Christ is the Savior and the Lord of Life. It is a person giving their life over to Jesus. It is casting oneself upon Jesus as Savior and Lord. We must realize that Jesus is the Resurrection and the Life. Jesus is alive. Jesus is both in us and all around us. Our faith is living and alive in us. All believers are in constant communion and fellowship with Jesus Christ. We must have a heartfelt love for Christ. Will you let Jesus in today like Mary and Martha? This time is NOW!

Ponder your Thoughts

Real Love

John 3:16. "For God so loved the world that He gave His only begotten Son, that whosoever believes in Him (Jesus Christ) shall not perish but have everlasting life."

This verse reveals the heart and *purpose* of God. God gave His only begotten Son, Jesus Christ, as an offering on the cross at Calvary. The Gospel of John begins with a poetic hymn that tells the story of Jesus's origin, mission, and function. John says that Jesus is the incarnated Word of God, bringing "grace and truth," replacing the law given by Moses, and making God known in the world. In John 1:17 says "For the law was given by Moses, *but* grace and truth came by Jesus Christ."

Salvation is not from yourself or anything you've done, but the gift of God." Salvation, therefore, is a gift of grace from God. When a person accepts the gift of salvation, he or she is said to be justified — made acceptable before (or made right with) God.

God's plan was always to use Old Testament sacrifices as a temporary measure, pointing towards the eventual ministry of the Messiah. Psalm 40:6 (Sacrifice and offering thou didst not desire; mine ears hast thou opened: burnt offering and sin offering hast thou not required.) was quoted to show how God's intent for His will involves a physical body, not offerings. The scriptures clearly point out that animal sacrifices could never fully cleanse man from sin, nor could they change us from the inside (Hebrews 9:8). The new covenant which god promised was to be in each person's heart and mind (Hebrews 9:8-10). "[8]The Holy Ghost this signifying, that the way into the holiest of all was not yet made manifest, while as the first tabernacle was yet standing: [9]Which was a figure for the time then present, in which were offered both gifts and sacrifices, that could not make him that did the service perfect, as pertaining to the conscience; [10]Which stood only in meats and drinks, and divers washings, and carnal ordinances, imposed on them until the time of reformation." The new covenant which God promised was to be in each person's heart and mind (Hebrews 8:7-13). "7 For if that first covenant had been faultless, then should no place have been sought for the second. 8 For finding fault with them, he saith, Behold, the days come, saith the Lord, when I will make a new covenant with the house of Israel and with the house of Judah: 9 Not according to the covenant that I made with their fathers in the day when I took them by the hand to lead them out of the land of Egypt; because they continued not in my covenant, and I regarded them not, saith the Lord. 10 For this is the covenant that I will make with the house of Israel after those days, saith the Lord; I will put my laws into their mind, and write them in their hearts: and I will be to them a God, and they shall be to me a people: 11 And they shall not teach every man his neighbour, and every man his brother, saying, Know the Lord: for all shall know me, from the least to the greatest. 12 For I will be merciful to their unrighteousness, and their sins and their iniquities will I remember no more. 13 In that he saith, A new covenant, he hath made the first old. Now that which decayeth and waxeth old is ready to vanish away." Animal blood was only able to atone for ceremonial issues, not to solve our deepest problems of sin. Jesus' sacrifice, on the other hand, obtains what not to solve our deepest problems of sin. Jesus' sacrifice, on the other hand, obtains what animal blood never could. Instead of being offered over and over, Jesus was sacrificed "once for animal blood never could. Instead of being offered over and over, Jesus was sacrificed "once for all." If animal sacrifices could have obtained that salvation, there would have been no need to repeat them (Hebrews 10:1-2). For the law having a shadow of good things to come, and not the very image of the things, can never with those sacrifices which they offered year by year continually make the comers thereunto perfect. ²For then would they not have ceased to be offered? because that the worshippers once purged should have had no more conscience of sins. The very fact that priest offered the same sacrifices over and over was proof that God never intended them to full pay for sin. Our "sanctification" comes only by the blood of Christ, not the sacrifice of animals.

We must believe! To believe means to have a sure conviction that Jesus Christ is God's only begotten Son. We must also realize that Jesus is the *only* Savior for Humanity. There must be a self-surrendering fellowship and obedience to Jesus Christ. We must have an assured trust and faith in Jesus Christ as our Savior.

What is *perish*? The dreadful reality of burning in hell! Who wants to go to hell? The Bible lets us know that we do have a choice. "Choose ye this day who you will serve," man or Jesus? Choose eternal life with Jesus Christ. *Choose eternal life with Jesus Christ!* This is the gift bestowed upon us when we are believers of Jesus Christ. God loves us and He has a plan for us. God promises a life free from the power of sin. Without the new birth no one can receive the new birth in Christ Jesus. New life comes through repentance of sin, turning to God, and putting your faith in Jesus Christ as your Lord and Savior. The Bible says, "God loved the world that He gave His one and only begotten Son (Jesus Christ), that whosoever believes shall not perish but have eternal life." (John 3:16)

Jesus said, "I came that they might have life and have it more abundantly." (John 10:10) – a complete life full of purpose. But here is the problem with humans. Humans are sinful and separated from God. We have all done, thought, or said bad things, which the Bible calls sin. The Bible says, "All have sinned and fallen short of the glory of God." (Romans 3:23) This is bad news! But we have the good news! Would you like to receive God's forgiveness today? God sent his Son, Jesus Christ, to die for our sins on Calvary's Cross. Jesus died in our place so we could have a relationship with God and be with Him forever.

"God demonstrates His love towards us, in that while we were yet sinners, Christ died for us" (Romans 5:8). "But it did not end with His death on the cross. Jesus rose again on the third day and He still lives! "Christ died for our sins…He was buried, He was raised on the third day, according to the Scriptures." ("For I delivered to you as of first importance what I also received, that Christ died for our sins according to the Scriptures, **4**and that He was buried, and that He was raised on the third day according to the Scriptures, **5**and that He appeared to Cephas, then to the twelve." (1 Corinthians 15:3-4.) "And He was received up into heaven and seated on the right hand of God." "Now when *Jesus* was risen early the first *day* of the week, he appeared first to Mary Magdalene, out of whom he had cast seven devils." (Mark 16:19).

Jesus is the only way to God. Jesus said, "I am the way, the truth, and the life. No one comes unto the Father, but through Me (Jesus Christ)" Jesus saith unto him, I am the way, the truth, and the life: no man cometh unto the Father, but by me. (John 14:6). We cannot *earn* salvation. We are saved by God's grace when we have faith in His Son, Jesus Christ, as our Lord and Savior. All you must do is believe that you are a sinner and that Christ died for our sins. Ask for His forgiveness. Then we must turn from our sins. This is call repentance. Repent for the Kingdom of God is at hand. Repent ye *this* day. The time is *now*. Tomorrow is not promised. Jesus Christ knows us and loves us.

What matters to Jesus is the attitude of our hearts – and our honesty! We suggest praying the following prayer.

Dear Lord Jesus, I know that I am a sinner, and I ask for Your forgiveness. I believe You died for my sins and rose from the dead. I turn from my sins and invite You to come into my heart and life. I want to trust and follow You as my Lord and Savior. Save me Lord Jesus. I receive you now as my Lord and Savorl!

Real Love. Remember, without the new birth, no one can have eternal life. New life comes through repentance of one's sin, turning to God, and putting one's faith in Jesus Christ as their Lord and Savior. The Bible says, "For God so loved the world that He gave His only begotten Son, that whosoever believes in Him, shall not perish but have eternal life." John 3:16.

The Scroll of Life – Deacon Andrew Jackson & Ora Dee Buckley
Andrew Jackson Buckley was born on July 26, 1920 to Lonzo and Amanda (Hall) Buckley in West Enterprise, Mississippi. He was united in marriage to Ora Dee "O'Bell" Johnson on August 13, 1935 in Quitman, Mississippi. Ora was born on March 5, 1923 to Warren and Ella (Andrew) Johnson in Enterprise, Mississippi. After 50 years of marriage, they have both gone on to be with the Lord. Ora slipped away to eternity on August 3, 1992 and seven years later, in a twinkling of an eye Andrew left us on April 2, 1999 at his residence in Racine, Wisconsin.

Andrew accepted Christ at the early age of eight years and was baptized in 1928 at Fellowship Baptist Church in West Enterprise, Mississippi. Fellowship was a little church house where everyone in the community gathered weekly to praise God, and to was baptized at Fellowship under the leadership of Reverend Barlow. Andrew had his eyes on the love of his life, Ora Dee Johnson. Andrew and Ora grew up together on the countryside of Enterprise, Mississippi. At an early age, Andrew was determined that he proposed marriage; he was 18 and Ora was 15 years old. They gathered their friends and relatives, including Annie Bell, Ella, Madree, and Bernie King and were married at the Court House in Quitman, Mississippi. On the morning of August 13, 1935 at 11:00 am they became Mr. and Mrs. Andrew Buckley. They travelled down that dusty road from Enterprise to Quitman, Mississippi in Bernie's 1935 Ford to begin a life together with the gift of love for each other.

The family walked to Fellowship Missionary Baptist Church

every Sunday. Andrew and Ora were a dedicated Christian couple determined to raise a Christian family. They made their home an "old house" back in the woods and walked three to four miles one-way to church each Sunday. Rev. Longmeyer preached once a month after which they usually eat dinner at the church and fellowshipped with the other families. And the Lord said to their union of marriage, "be fruitful and multiply." Fruitful indeed, they were blessed with fifteen children in the following order. Those delivered by mid-wife Mahalia Simpson in Enterprise, Mississippi: Lydia Mae-1939 first born (died in 1965 in Racine, Wisconsin from a car accident on Durand Avenue; Ella Louise-1941 second born; Amanda Deloris-1943 third born; Eula Mae-1945 fourth born; and Annie Dee-1946 fifth born. Those delivered by Betty Buckley a mid-wife in Enterprise, Mississippi. Andrew Jackson-1948, the sixth born (still birth); Della Jane-1949 seventh born, Mary Ann-191951 eight born, (died July 2005); Johnny Mize-1952 nineth born (died of asthma in 1955); and Betty Sue-tenth born. After moving to Racine, Wisconsin the fruit continued to grow multiply. The other children were at born at St. Luke's Hospital in Racine by Medical Doctors. Wanda Kay-1956 the eleventh born; Willie Maze-1957 the twelfth born; Shirley Lee-1960 thirteenth born; Joseph Charles-1961 fourteenth born and Anthony Terry-1963 fifteenth born (died of a fatal gun shot wound on January 2, 1989). Honor and glory to a virtuous woman, Ora gave birth to all her children by natural birth!

Andrew & Ora Johnson Buckley Scroll of Life

Andrew Buckley always believed that his children and wife should go everywhere with him. God had blessed him overwhelmingly with beautiful daughters. Andrew was always very protective of his girls and Ora kept them beautiful in lace dresses made by her hands; she was a very devoted wife and mother. She tended to the daily chores, washing, ironing, taking care of the children, the garden and tended to the hogs and chickens. God blessed Ora with the gift of cooking, everything figure licking good! She measured all the ingredients by hand (no measuring cup needed). Similarly, she the gift of making any plant grow. She was an avid lover of green plants and grew the biggest collard green in the world.

Andrew always has zeal to be the head of his large family. Hard work was no stranger to his hands. He owned a timber business in 1945 with 9 employees. Bennie Kirk, a white man, was very instrumental in Andrew's business savvy. They cut pulp wood and transported it by railroad boxcars to Mobile, Alabama. Andrew had the unique opportunity of owning a timber business in the Deep South which was rare. Considering the times and being a Negro Man. Due to the shortage at that time, Andrew had to close his business and he went to work for Bennie Kirk; Andrew was aid $6.00 a day. Andrew was gifted with skillful hands and a sharp mind; he also, was an avid baseball player and singer.

When work became scare in Mississippi, Andrew determined to be the head of his household, prayerfully decided to go north to find work. Go North, Go North, the land flowing with milk and honey. In February 1955 Andrew and Mr. Wainwright traveled to Racine, Wisconsin where he was hired at the J.I. Case Company. Later, in April 1965 Warren Johnson, Ora's father, drove her and eight children to Racine, Wisconsin in a small 1940 Ford Studebaker. The family moved into a two-bedroom house on Packard avenue, but soon thereafter Andrew was laid off from JI. Case Company. It was hard times; everyone worked in the onion fields to help supplement the family income and buy food. But the Lord blessed and after a short time, Andrew was hired at bell City as "Stand Grind" Operator. Years later, the company was sold to the Racine Steel Company. Andrew worked at this company faithfully and never missed a day from work, except for one episode of illness. He retired in July 1982 with an exemplary work record!

As the head of his hose, Andrew led the family to the Lord. Andrew and Ora joined the Greater Mount Eagle Baptist Church in 1961, under the leadership of the Rev. E. E Woods. On January 19, 1974, Andrew was ordained as a Deacon by Pastor Mark Toles of the Second Missionary Baptist Church in Kenosha, Wisconsin. At that time, Pastor Charles Thornhill was the pastor the Greater Mount Eagle Baptist Church. Deacon Buckley was a faithful and dedicated member of the Greater Mount Eagle Baptist Church. He had perfect attendance in Sunday School, weekly worship services and bible study. He also was a dedicated member of the Male chorus. And of course, he never missed a business meeting of the church. Deacon Buckley mirrored his worship of God by being good and faithful member of the church as well by being a faithful servant of the Lord. Ora was a faithful member of the church as well; contributing to church special events and fellowships and supporting her children who labored in the ministry. We can honestly say that Andrew and Ora Buckley were good and faithful servants of God in a unique way; they continued to work whit it was day.

Ora's true ministry was in the house that she made a home for her immediate family and those in the neighborhood whom she loved dearly. She spent most of life at home as a homemaker, caring for Andrew, her 12 children and grandchildren, washing clothes with a ringer washer daily, and tending to her garden She was devoted to the misfortunate and down trodden people that needed a "mother's love," which she gave unconditionally. She loved people genuinely and unselfishly. Even with all her responsibilities at home, Ora pitched in and worked outside the home as a cook for the Breakers' restaurant. This was extremely hard for us, but we can remember ought into the car to go and pick he up from work and Mama always bought us treats; sch an endearing love! As the y ears passed and with the slaying of Ora's youngest son, terry, she became weary and v tremendously. However, the legacy of her ministry of helping people, lives on through her children. God gave us a special mother that exemplified the meaning of "family" that can only be experienced through the anointing and guidance of the Holy spirit. On August 3, 1992, God called his good and faithful servant home from labor to reward.

A Tribute of Love

God said, "Honor thy father and thy mother." We give tribute and praises to God for these special gifts of love, our parents Deacon Andrew Jackson and Ora Belle Buckley for their lives of splendor and special beauty that can only be given by our Heavenly Father. Daddy and Mama, we love you and thank you for being our steadfast, unmovable, abounding in faith mother and father, grandparents, uncle, aunt, deacon and man and woman of god. You were always committed to your beliefs and morals that exemplify the epitome of what godly African American parents should stand for. We salute your memories, thy good and faithful servants. We come together to simply say, Daddy and Mama you were our Heroes. Praise God for making a man and woman like our parents!

Ponder your Thoughts

Ponder your Thoughts

CPSIA information can be obtained
at www.ICGtesting.com
Printed in the USA
BVHW031116231120
593598BV00011BA/23/J